SCHOOL BUS SAFETY

Written by **Lieutenant Becky Coyle**

Illustrated by **juanbjuan oliver**

and **Elmira Eskandari**

An Introduction to Rules and Safety on the School Bus

SCHOOL SAFETY

School Resource Officer Approved

For John, Timmy, Selah, and Amanda.

A special thank you to Dr. Melonye Lowe for encouraging me to follow my dreams and my dear friend Terry Cline. You will always be my favorite bus driver!

And for Sandy Webster, in celebration of 40 years at Scales Elementary School.

www.FlowerpotPress.com
PAB-0909-0377
ISBN: 978-1-4867-3005-6
Made in China/Fabriqué en Chine

Hi, my name is Becky. I am a police lieutenant and school resource officer. I love teaching children just like you the importance of being safe while they are playing and learning at school.

Sometimes it is hard to understand why you have to practice drills and follow school rules, but being prepared is an important part of keeping your school safe. Your teachers, school officer, classmates, and even YOU play an important role in ensuring that your school is a place where you can do all of the things that you love to do! By working together and following the rules, we can accomplish so much!

For more information, discussion topics, and activities, visit my website!

www.Cops4Schools.com.

Stay safe,
Lieutenant Becky Coyle

"I'm so excited! I can hardly wait!

The first day of school is going to be great!"

Nina was snoring and snuggled in deep
when she heard her mom's voice disrupting her sleep.

"Nina!" Mom said. "There's no time to rest!
We're running behind! Wake up and get dressed!"

She climbed out of bed and jumped to her feet
and ran down the stairs for something to eat.

She crunched her last bite, slurped up every drop,
then raced out the door and toward her bus stop.

"Oh no!" Nina huffed. "I'm almost too late!"

She waved as she ran and shouted, "PLEASE, WAIT!"

Her friends cried out, "STOP!" but she'd gone too far.

She ran through the street and in front of a car!

"That was so scary! I'm glad you're not hurt.

When crossing a street, we must stay alert.

Always STOP where it's safe, and LOOK left and right.

Then LISTEN for cars that might be out of sight.

Rules are important for danger prevention.

They help keep us safe. We must pay attention!"

Nina liked learning rules to help her through the day,
so the other kids shared them as they went on their way.

"Don't be in a rush,
but try not to be late.
Stay twelve giant steps
from the curb while you wait!"

"Don't walk toward the bus
while it's still pulling in.
It must come to a stop
before boarding begins."

"When climbing the stairway,
it's easy to slip.
Please use the handrail
and keep a firm grip."

"When our bus is moving,
stay in your seat.
Keep main aisles clear
and bags at your feet."

"If the bus windows
are down when you ride,
keep your head and your arms
safely inside."

"The bus can get noisy when there's a big crowd.
Be polite and respectful. Don't get too loud!"

"When you reach your stop,
stand up,
get in line,
then patiently exit one at a time."

"Great job, everyone!
You sure know your rules.
Thanks for the fun.
Have a great day at school!"

"See you tomorrow!"